THE
POCKET

DISCOVER
PARIS

Published in 2025
by Gemini Gift Books
Part of Gemini Books Group

Based in Woodbridge and London

Marine House, Tide Mill Way,
Woodbridge, Suffolk IP12 1AP
United Kingdom

www.geminibooks.com

Text and Design © 2025 Gemini Gift Books Ltd
Part of the Gemini Pockets series

Text by Becky Freeth

Cover illustration by Grace Helmer

ISBN 978-1-80247-305-6

A CIP catalogue record for this book is available from the British Library.

Disclaimer: The book is a guidebook purely for information and entertainment purposes only. All trademarks, individual and company names, brand names, registered names, quotations, celebrity names, logos, dialogues and catchphrases used or cited in this book are the property of their respective owners. The publisher does not assume and hereby disclaims any liability to any party for any loss, damage or disruption caused by errors or omissions, whether such errors or omissions result from negligence, accident or any other cause. This book is an unofficial and unauthorized publication by Gemini Gift Books Ltd and has not been licensed, approved, sponsored or endorsed by any other person or entity.

Manufacturer's EU Representative: Eurolink Compliance Limited, 25 Herbert Place, Dublin, D02 AY86, Republic of Ireland. admin@eurolink-europe.ie

Printed in China

10 9 8 7 6 5 4 3 2 1

MIX
Paper | Supporting
responsible forestry
FSC™ C017606
www.fsc.org

Picture Credits: Shutterstock: nataniki / 6, 21, 26, 38, 70; Wiktoria Matynia / 11, 19; GooseFrol / 13, 15, 17, 28, 32, 34, 46; Katsiaryna Pleshakova / 25, 43, 61, 77, 97, 100, 106, 111, 114; bebe3 / 44, 79, 86, 98; Anastacia – azzzya / 50, 52, 56; Anna Sol / 53, 64, 72, 83, 117; Yevheniia Lytvynovych / 104, 108; Romanova Ekaterina / 40, 41, 48, 49, 74, 75, 90, 91. Freepik: 120, 126.

THE POCKET

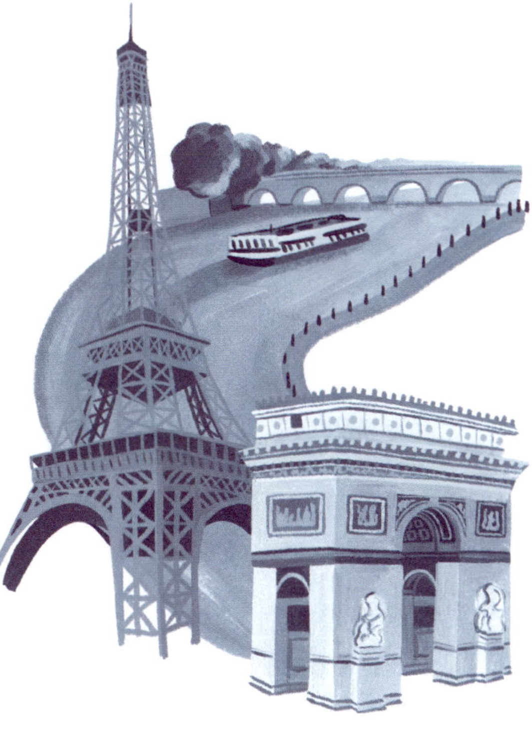

DISCOVER PARIS

G:

CONTENTS

City of lights. City of art, history, fashion and, of course, romance. Whatever brought you here, you will find the best of it in Paris.

It's easy to explore this city on foot, hopping off buses at iconic attractions (Notre-Dame, Sainte-Chapelle, the Panthéon) or riding the Metro, crossing off bucket-list attractions faster than you can say: "Arc de Triomphe!"

But if you have more time, while away your hours in the Louvre. Sail the Seine. Face onto Rue des Halles on a café terrace watching elegant Parisians float through the fashion districts. Eat a baguette, or several.

However you pass your time, let this pocket guide be your handy companion, making sure you don't miss a single highlight of the French capital.

"Paris is always a good idea."

Julia Ormond as Sabrina,
in *Sabrina* (1995)

The Seine & the Snail

The famous Seine River cuts the French capital into two halves. The right bank (Rive Droite) makes up two thirds of the city and the remainder is on the left bank (Rive Gauche).

Paris is further divided into 20 arrondissements (or rounds) that spiral outwards into a snail-shell shape from the 1st in the centre, clockwise around to the 20th.

LE PREMIER

1st Arrondissement

HIGHLIGHTS

The Louvre
Forum des Halles
The Ritz Paris
Musée des Arts Décoratifs
Musée Grévin
Musée de l'Orangerie

AREAS TO EXPLORE

Palais-Royal & Jardins
Place Vendôme
Les Halles

FREE EXPERIENCES

✲ Take a selfie at Vendôme Column
✲ Enjoy street food at Les
  Halles fresh-food market
✲ Picnic and statue-hunt
  at Tuileries Garden
✲ Browse underground shops
  at Carrousel du Louvre
✲ Window shop on Rue
  Saint-Honoré

MARAIS AND ÎLE DE LA CITÉ

2nd, 3rd & 4th Arrondissements

HIGHLIGHTS

Notre-Dame Cathedral
Sainte-Chapelle
Musée Picasso
Maison de Victor Hugo
Centre Pompidou
Musée de la Chasse et de la Nature

AREAS TO EXPLORE

Pletzl
Marais
Île de la Cité
Île Saint-Louis

FREE EXPERIENCES

✽ Cross over Pont Neuf
  bridge to Île de la Cité

✽ Discover the underground
  arcades at Grands Boulevards

✽ Time travel at the oldest square
  in Paris, Place des Vosges

✽ Photograph rare flowers
  at Marché aux Fleurs

✽ Capture the quirky exterior of
  59 Rivoli and catch a free exhibit

LATIN QUARTER & SAINT-GERMAIN-DES-PRÉS

5th, 6th & 7th Arrondissements

HIGHLIGHTS

Eiffel Tower
Musée d'Orsay
The Panthéon
Hôtel des Invalides
Musée Rodin
Boulevard St-Germain
Pont des Arts
Champ de Mars

AREAS TO EXPLORE

Latin Quarter
Saint Germain-des-Prés
Luxembourg Quarter

FREE EXPERIENCES

✻ Amble along Rue Mouffetard

✻ Peruse admission-free art at Musée de la Sculpture en Plein Air

✻ Explore the nature trails at Jardin des Plantes

✻ Picnic inside Jardin du Luxembourg with children

✻ Enjoy amazing views of the Eiffel Tower from the ground on Promenade Marie de Roumanie

✻ Shop at Le Bon Marché

CHAMPS-ÉLYSÉES

8th & 9th Arrondissements

HIGHLIGHTS

Arc de Triomphe
Grand Palais
Petit Palais
Palais de la Découverte
Opéra Garnier
Théâtre Mogador

AREAS TO EXPLORE

Haussmann Saint-Lazare
Place Charles de Gaulle
Avenue des Champs-Élysées
Avenue Montaigne

FREE EXPERIENCES

✽ Shop on "The Golden Triangle"
✽ Cross the Seine at
  Pont Alexandre III
✽ Have a coffee on Place
  de la Concorde
✽ View the window displays
  at Galeries Lafayette
✽ Browse through Printemps
✽ Marvel at the Église
  de la Madeleine

CANAL SAINT-MARTIN

10th to 16th Arrondissements

HIGHLIGHTS

Gare du Nord
Gare de l'Est
Opéra Bastille
Musée Édith Piaf
Les Catacombes
Montparnasse Tower
Observation Deck
Fondation Louis Vuitton
Palais de Tokyo

AREAS TO EXPLORE

Strasbourg-Saint-Denis
Rue Oberkampf
Rue du Faubourg Saint-Antoine
Montparnasse
Trocadéro

FREE EXPERIENCES

❋ Visit Place de la République
❋ Watch boats on the Canal
  Saint-Martin trail
❋ Walk Coulée Verte René-
  Dumont (similar to New York's
  High Line) from Place de la
  Bastille to Bois de Vincennes
❋ Tour Île aux Cygnes island
❋ Catch the Marché Richard Lenoir

MONTMARTRE & BEYOND

17th to 20th Arrondissements

HIGHLIGHTS

Sacré-Cœur
Montmartre
La Cité des Sciences
et de l'Industrie
Moulin Rouge
Parc de la Villette
Place de la Nation

AREAS TO EXPLORE

Montmartre
Belleville
Batignolles

FREE EXPERIENCES

✳ Catch a film at Cinéma en Plein Air at Parc de la Villette in summer

✳ Enjoy food on the steps of Sacré-Cœur

✳ Chase waterfalls at Parc des Buttes-Chaumont

✳ Admire the flowers at La Cité des Fleurs

✳ Stop for coffee on Rue des Martyrs

✳ Photograph the Love Wall, where "I love you" is written in 312 languages

"What an immense impression Paris made upon me. It is the most extraordinary place in the world!"

Charles Dickens,
writing about his first visit in 1844

Let the Games Begin (Again)

Fencing at the Grand Palais. Skateboarding on the Place de la Concorde. Beach volleyball underneath the Eiffel Tower.

The 2024 Paris Olympics commandeered some of the city's most prized venues as they hosted the Games exactly a century after the first Parisian Olympics.

The event drew in 1.7 million international visitors and was watched around the world by an unprecedented number of sports fans.

CHAPTER ONE

SIGHT-SEEING

Did You Know?

One look at the Eiffel Tower, illuminated by 20,000 light bulbs at night, and you'll understand why the capital's glittering nickname as The City of Light has prevailed.

But did you know Paris was one of the first cities to adopt street lighting in 1667?

Not only did it make the nights safer, it enveloped the city in a warm and welcoming glow, which attracted its favourable new nickname along with a wealth of visitors.

"A walk about Paris will provide lessons in history, beauty, and in the point of life."

Thomas Jefferson (1743–1826)

Eiffel Tower

BEST FOR: ROMANCE
AREA: CHAMP DE MARS

Don't Miss... Tickets to climb the staircase inside. Advance bookings open around 60 days before.

Did You Know...? It was once the tallest building in the world, until the Chrysler Building was completed in 1930.

Insider Tip... Get off the Metro at Trocadéro for a surprising view from the ground.

A cultural icon and a national institution,
the Eiffel Tower is among the most instantly
recognizable landmarks on the planet.

No matter how many times you've seen
the image immortalized in print, its
scale and magnificence are something
you have to witness in person. If
only to take your own pictures.

It's a romantic symbol of Paris in its
"beautiful era" (La Belle Époque,
page 116) – a period of optimism and
economic prosperity in French history –
and is unsurprisingly one of the most popular
places in the world for marriage proposals.

The Eiffel Tower in Numbers

❊ The attraction opened in **1889**.

❊ Its bones (the beams and bolts) were built by **150 factory workers**.

❊ The structure is held together by **2,500,000 rivets** (bolts).

❊ Construction took just **two years, two months and five days**.

❊ It stands at **1,083 feet** tall (330 meters) with **674 steps** between floors.

❊ **Seven million** people visit each year.

❊ It has its own Michelin-star restaurant, Jules Verne, **410 feet (125 meters)** up.

"I ought to be jealous of the tower. She is more famous than I am."

Gustave Eiffel, French civil engineer and designer of the Eiffel Tower (1832–1923)

Arc de Triomphe

**BEST FOR: A HISTORY LESSON
AREA: PLACE CHARLES DE GAULLE**

Don't Miss... The small but interesting
museum located inside.

Did You Know...? An eternal flame
is rekindled every night in tribute
to an unknown soldier who died on
the site during World War I.

Insider Tip... For an unobstructed view,
visit on the first Sunday of December, when
cars are banned on the Champs-Élysées.

Construction started when Napoleon Bonaparte promised that he would march his soldiers home through the Arc de Triomphe when war in France was over. But the emperor never lived to see peace in Paris.

Finished 15 years after his death, the landmark is a symbol of victory in the city for the wars won under his leadership. It stands triumphant at the western terminus of the Champs-Élysées with images of soldiers on each of the four corners.

As magnificent as it is to travel under the triumphal arch, you can also climb the 284 steps to reach the top, where the reward is a spectacular view of the city.

Notre-Dame

BEST FOR: THE POST-RESTORATION ERA
AREA: ÎLE DE LA CITÉ

Don't Miss... The 14th-century statue
known as the Virgin of the Pillar,
which survived the 2019 blaze.

Did You Know...? The Olympic Bell rung
by victorious athletes at the recent Paris
Games is now housed in one of the towers.

Insider Tip... Visit after 5.30pm
for quieter entry – you may even
overhear the Vespers Service.

Over 600 years since it was
constructed, Notre-Dame cathedral
is more resplendent than ever.

In December 2024, this icon of the city
reopened following a painstaking five-year
restoration project. The original medieval
cathedral took two centuries to build, but
a catastrophic fire tore down the roof
and spire in one fateful night in 2019.

When plans were made to save it, the
suggestion was to modernize the landmark.
Instead, the restoration is as loyal to the
original as possible, maintaining some of the
world's most recognizable heritage features.

Sainte-Chapelle

BEST FOR: GOOSE BUMPS
AREA: ÎLE DE LA CITÉ

Don't Miss... Classical concerts
held during the winter months.
The acoustics are astonishing.

Did You Know...? Each piece of the
stained glass tells a story from the Old
and New Testaments of the Bible.

Insider Tip... There is an app
that helps visitors identify and
understand each unique window.

Pictures could never do justice to the awe-inspiring Sainte-Chapelle. Standing in the light of 1,113 iridescent panels – the world's most extensive collection of 13th-century stained glass – is an experience you need to witness for yourself.

The holy chapel was originally built to house relics of Jesus Christ. However, Paris' most beautiful church has done well to survive two fires, one flood and the French Revolution (page 54) in its turbulent history, so some have understandably been relocated.

Among the 19 precious relics once kept here, the most important was the "Crown of Thorns", which is now held at Notre-Dame for safe-keeping.

The Panthéon

**BEST FOR: HISTORY OF FRENCH FIGURES
AREA: LATIN QUARTER**

Don't Miss... 360-degree views of the city from the colonnade at the top.

Did You Know...? It was completed just as the French Revolution broke out.

Insider Tip... Marie Curie was the first woman to be "Panthéonized" for her own achievements.

To visit the Panthéon is to be in the presence of greatness. It's been the final resting place for many influential French citizens, writers, politicians and scientists including eminent author Victor Hugo and the educator Louis Braille. You can pay homage in the vaults known as the crypt.

At ground level, you may spend more time looking up than looking around. The magnificent main domes of the temple resemble that of St Paul's Cathedral in London, but the architecture was originally inspired by the Panthéon in Rome.

Sightseeing From the Seine

One of the most idyllic ways to see
the landmarks of Paris is by boat.

Tick the Louvre, the Eiffel Tower and Notre-
Dame off your must-see list in under an
hour, away from the traffic and crowds.

Aside from catching the obvious sights,
the lesser-spotted Statue of Liberty replica
on Île-aux-Cygnes is one-such monument
you might not have made the journey to.

By night, the water tours have a more
romantic atmosphere. To add to the dazzle
of Paris's city lights, you can upgrade
to a champagne and dinner cruise, or
dance to live music under the stars.

Best Water Tours

* Illuminations night tour
* Dinner & dancing
* Tour of Old Paris
* River & canal tour
* Lunch cruise
* Private boat (premium)
* Bus boat (affordable)
* New Year's cruise
* Champagne tasting
* Romantic cruise

CHAPTER TWO

MUSEUMS & GALLERIES

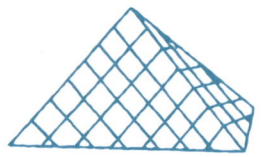

The Louvre

BEST FOR: THE BUCKET LIST
AREA: ÎLE DE LA CITÉ

Don't Miss... Musée des Arts Décoratifs:
the most extensive holdings of design
and decorative arts in the world.

Did You Know...? It would take more
than three months to view all of the
art individually (even if you spent
just 30 seconds looking at each!).

Insider Tip... The temporary
exhibitions are often the highlights.

No guide to Paris would be complete
without a dedication to the Louvre, the
world's most-visited museum, attracting
an unbelievable 8 million people a year.

It was Napoleon who turned this magnificent
Renaissance-style palace – once home to
Charles V and Louis XIV – into a museum;
intended, he once said, to house all of France's
"riches in the field of art and science".

From a humble collection of 12 paintings
in 1793, it now displays 35,000 works of
art, including (of course) the *Mona Lisa*.

Musée Picasso

BEST FOR: ARDENT FANS
AREA: MARAIS

Don't Miss... The room of portraits, showcasing a unique and inimitable part of Picasso's artistic style.

Did You Know...? Picasso first came to Paris in 1900, when the city was the "art capital of Europe".

Insider Tip... Take your time here. It is one of the quietest museums to enjoy.

It's hard to believe that Pablo Picasso produced 147,800 pieces of art during his storied life. That's roughly 2,500 pieces for every one of his adult years.

Here at the Musée Picasso, the largest collection of his Paris works is displayed at the historical Hôtel Salé, a French mansion built in 1659.

Picasso fans will love walking through the artist's life, painting by painting, sculpture by sculpture: through drawings, prints and ceramics, all displayed in chronological order. Enriching the detail of his life story are the newspaper clippings, personal poems and photographs displayed here with them.

Grand Palais or Petit Palais?

If you have just one afternoon in Paris, how do you choose between the two sister galleries that vie for your attention, just opposite each other? Each could take a whole afternoon to explore.

Both the Grand Palais and Petit Palais were designed to reflect "the glory of France" during the 1900 World Fair, an event to celebrate the country's achievements. Some 50 million international guests attended and the two magnificent Palais buildings were a star attraction.

Grand Palais

BEST FOR:

Architecture: It's called "Grand" for a reason. The big sister museum is a marvel of stately architecture from La Belle Époque era (page 116).

History: This grand event space annually hosts everything from Chanel fashion shows to the world's largest indoor ice rink.

Petit Palais

BEST FOR:

A peaceful pit stop: The Petit Palais café is one of the calmest and most exquisite eateries in the Champs-Élysées district.

Free activity: Entrance to the public exhibitions is free of charge. Come for the art, stay for the beautiful grounds.

Centre Pompidou

BEST FOR: MODERN ART & ARCHITECTURE
AREA: LES HALLES

Don't Miss... The view from the top after taking the external escalator.

Did You Know...? The building was the brainchild of French president Georges Pompidou, who died before it opened.

Insider Tip... Locals like to enjoy food in the courtyards in front of the museum.

This unique hub of modern arts and culture was unlike anything in Paris when it arrived in the late 1970s.

Curiously, the Centre Pompidou was built to look "inside out" with colourful exposed ducts and utility pipes decorating the façade. Its unusual aspect against a landscape of 18th- and 19th-century architecture represented precisely what it intended: the future of Paris.

If you can drag yourself away from the exterior, inside you will find two cinemas, a library and shops. By far, the biggest draw is the Musée National d'Art Moderne, second only to New York's Museum of Modern Art with its huge contemporary art collection.

Hôtel des Invalides

BEST FOR: MILITARY PRESTIGE
AREA: 7TH ARRONDISSEMENT

Don't Miss... Quiet relaxation on the well-manicured grounds – especially during summer months.

Did You Know...? Napoleon's tomb is nested within five other coffins, like a Russian doll.

Insider Tip... For the best view of the building and gardens, approach from the Seine.

A fitting tribute to fallen heroes of France, the grand Hôtel des Invalides – with its gilded dome and expansive lawns – was originally constructed as a hospital to care for war veterans during the 17th century.

Naturally, Napoleon was buried here. History lovers visit from all over the world to see his majestic tomb resting directly beneath the illustrious chapel dome.

Today, the huge property is the home of an unmissable military museum, Musée de l'Armée, renowned for one of the largest collections of arms and armoury in the world.

Vive la Revolution!

In 1789, an army of insurgents within Paris stormed the Bastille prison with weapons looted from Hôtel des Invalides (page 52) to protest against the French monarchy. An uprising had been brewing in the city for two years as the wealth gap widened between the rich and poor.

Tensions finally erupted into a French Revolution that July, which – although deadly – was effective in overthrowing the king and increasing the freedom of the people.

"You can't escape
the past in Paris,
and yet what's so
wonderful about
it is that the past
and present
intermingle so
intangibly that
it doesn't seem
to burden."

Poet Allen Ginsberg (1926–1997)

Musée d'Orsay

**BEST FOR: A JOURNEY THROUGH ART
AREA: INVALIDES & SAINT-GERMAIN-
DES-PRÉS**

Don't Miss... Edgar Degas' moving
sculpture *Little Dancer Aged Fourteen*.

Did You Know...? The original Gare d'Orsay,
which houses the Musée d'Orsay, was
built for the World Fair in 1900.

Insider Tip... Visit in the early
morning to beat the crowds.

Step inside a magnificent converted railway station and go on a journey through Impressionism.

What was originally the world's first electrified train terminal, Gare d'Orsay, is now a lofty exhibition space saved from demolition by the idea to exhibit 19th-century art here.

Highlights of this impressive museum include world-famous paintings by Pierre-Auguste Renoir and Claude Monet. There is also a section dedicated to works by Van Gogh in his last two months of his life.

Build in time here to visit Café Campana in the light of the huge station clock window.

Fondation Louis Vuitton

BEST FOR: APPRECIATORS OF ARCHITECTURE
AREA: 16TH ARRONDISSEMENT

A short shuttle ride from the Arc de Triomphe, the Fondation Louis Vuitton museum is surely worth the journey for art lovers.

This remarkable glass exhibition house attracts over one million visitors every year with contemporary arts displays sourced from all over the world, as well as original pieces commissioned exclusively for the museum.

Did You Know?

The Fondation Louis Vuitton is said
to have cost around **£600 million**
($820 million) to construct – eight
times the original estimate.

Unveiled in 2014, the result is
a strikingly unique landmark,
which is a work of art in itself.

CHAPTER THREE

PARIS WITH CHILDREN

Palais de la Découverte

BEST FOR: YOUNG ADULTS
AREA: CHAMPS-ÉLYSÉES

Don't Miss... A special new section for two-to ten-year-olds called Palais des Enfants.

Did You Know...? This is the first major renovation in the building's (almost) 100-year history.

Insider Tip... The majority of exhibits are aimed at teens and their parents.

Not only was the Palais de la Découverte already one of the best-loved attractions in Paris for children and parents, the science museum has been undergoing some extensive renovations ready for a grand reopening in summer 2025.

The revamp includes new exhibitions and laboratories, aquariums, terrariums and a planetarium, all housed within the decadent west wing of the Grand Palais.

Here, young learners can discover science in all its forms including maths, physics, chemistry, biology, medicine and artificial intelligence (AI), even getting the chance to watch live experiments.

Parc de la Villette

BEST FOR: DAYS OUT
AREA: 19TH ARRONDISSEMENT

Don't Miss... The raised promenades
for unmatched views of the park.

Did You Know...? An estimated 10 million
people visit the park each year.

Insider Tip... The park is close to Paris Metro
stations: Corentin Cariou and Porte de Pantin.

Parc de la Villette is just far enough from the beaten track that tourists don't stumble across this paradise for children by chance. If you know, you know.

Many come here for Europe's largest science museum, La Cité des Sciences et de l'Industrie, not realizing how much the park itself has to offer, including a domed 3D cinema (La Géode) and playgrounds for every age group.

In summer, la Villette is buzzing with locals, thanks to an outdoor cinema, often showing family films on weekends, and the opening of child-friendly bathing pools that line the canal.

Musée Grévin

BEST FOR: STAR-STUDDED PARIS
AREA: MONTMARTRE

Don't Miss... Nights at the museum,
hosted once a month.

Did You Know...? Up to the minute waiting
times are displayed on the website all day.

Insider Tip... Guided tours include dressing
up and behind-the-scenes access.

What height is Dwayne "The Rock" Johnson? How big are Beyoncé's feet? There's only one place in Paris to get close enough to find out.

France's answer to Madame Tussauds, Musée Grévin, is a unique chance for face-to-face access to stars of sports, screen and entertainment with 200 waxworks of everyone from Louis XIV to the Paw Patrol.

Besides a camera roll full of celebrity selfies, children will leave with heads full of history, thanks to incredible immersive exhibits on Versailles and the liberation of France.

Muséum National d'Histoire Naturelle

BEST FOR: HISTORY OF LIFE ON EARTH
AREA: JARDIN DES PLANTES

Don't Miss... The palaeontology section.

Did You Know...? The grounds used to be for growing and studying medicinal plants.

Insider Tip... Make time to visit the gardens afterwards.

Just outside the hubbub of the city, set within the peaceful Jardin des Plantes, the National Museum of Natural History is the perfect place to lose yourself for an afternoon.

Even grown-ups will be craning their necks to see enormous life-size animals of our modern planet, arranged like a wild procession through this staggering 17th-century building. Bigger still are the prehistoric dinosaur skeletons, some 82 ft (25 m) long.

When you imagine these mammoth displays through the eyes of a child, you'll understand why this museum is one of the most prestigious in the world.

Jardin du Luxembourg

**BEST FOR: OLD-FASHIONED FUN
AREA: LATIN QUARTER**

Don't Miss... Any of the 108 magnificent statues around the gardens.

Did You Know...? Here in the middle of the city, the gardens hold an orchard and a beehive.

Insider Tip... Wise visitors bring baguettes and wine for a picnic.

A rare sight in a city as tightly packed as Paris, 56 unspoiled acres of gardens make up the enchanting Jardin du Luxembourg. The park and lakes were gifted to the children of Paris by Napoleon III during the 19th century and now offer whole afternoons-worth of joyful, low-cost games and pastimes for little ones.

There's a vast lake for sailing traditional model boats and a vintage carousel. You can even ride real ponies or race vintage peddle go-karts for unique ways to explore the grounds.

One highlight for all the family is the charming marionette theatre, Théâtre des Marionnettes, that's been drawing in crowds since 1933.

Best Parks...

...With Puppet Shows

❈ **Parc Monceau** (8th Arrondissement)

❈ **Parc Montsouris** (14th Arrondissement)

❈ **Parc du Champ de Mars** (7th Arrondissement)

❈ **Georges Brassens Park** (15th Arrondissement)

❈ **Parc Floral de Paris** (12th Arrondissement)

...With Merry-Go-Rounds

❈ **Parc de la Villette** (19th Arrondissement)

❈ **Jardin d'Acclimatation** (16th Arrondissement)

❈ **Jardins du Trocadéro** (16th Arrondissement)

❈ **Jardin des Plantes** (5th Arrondissement)

❈ **Jardin des Tuileries** (1st Arrondissement)

"Whoever does not visit Paris regularly will never really be elegant."

Honoré de Balzac,
Treatise on Elegant Living (1830)

Disneyland Paris

BEST FOR: MAGICAL ADVENTURES
AREA: MARNE-LA-VALLÉE

More people travel to Paris for the Disneyland
theme park than for the Louvre and Eiffel
Tower combined. But don't mistake this
for an afternoon of thrills in the capital,
as the park is not in Paris itself.

Still, it's within reach for a short trip, just
one hour outside the city, and the promise
of fun and enchantment for children – even
the young at heart – cannot be overstated.

The majestic Sleeping Beauty Castle is the
backdrop for "the happiest place on earth"
and the most iconic place to capture a selfie in
mouse ears before you start your adventure.

Once inside, buckle up for rides,
parades, fireworks, music, shops,
boat rides and more food than you
can shake a flashing glow stick at.

Did You Know?

Disneyland Paris was originally
called Euro Disney, however
tourists felt this linked too
much to the Euro currency
and had financial – not
magical – connotations, so
the name was changed a mere
two years after opening to
include the aspirational city.

Check out the lampposts
around Lake Disney and you'll
still see the original name!

CHAPTER FOUR

SHOPPING

"The shopping, the food, the views! Paris is a city that entrances us all – and I'm no exception."

Michael Kors, *Condé Nast Traveller*, September 2020

Fashion Showdown

Expensive custom-fitted fashion known as "haute couture" was born in the ateliers of Paris, when in 1858 Charles Frederick Worth became the first designer to showcase clothes on real women and not mannequins. Fashion shows quickly caught on.

Today, Paris is one of the "Big Four" fashion capitals of the world and twice a year, the world's finest models, designers, photographers and spectators shut down New York, London, Paris and Milan for Fashion Week, a four-day showcase of the latest high-fashion designs.

Avenue Montaigne

BEST FOR: HIGH FASHION
AREA: CHAMPS-ÉLYSÉES

Don't Miss... The recently reopened Christian Dior store, now with a café and museum inside.

Did You Know...? The street is named after the French Renaissance writer, Michel de Montaigne.

Insider Tip... Hidden just behind the high street is an enchanting secret garden café called La Cour Jardin.

Lined with every designer store you can dream of, Avenue Montaigne is the sleek and shiny side of the Triangle d'Or (the "Golden Triangle") shopping district in Paris.

At either end, it's flanked by Avenues Georges V and the Champs-Élysées, lining you up for an unbeatable day of luxury shopping.

Chanel, Louis Vuitton, Gucci, Prada and Saint Laurent have boutiques on this wide, walkable shopping street. The star attraction is the Christian Dior flagship at 30 Avenue Montaigne where the designer showcased his first collection in 1947.

Avenue des Champs-Élysées

BEST FOR: SIGHTS & SHOPPING
AREA: CHAMPS-ÉLYSÉES

Don't Miss... Tuilerie Gardens. Start at Arc de Triomphe and walk the avenue toward Place de la Concorde.

Did You Know...? Louis Vuitton's Champs-Élysées store is the most-visited in the world!

Insider Tip... Don't eat on Avenue des Champs-Élysées. Locals will tell you the restaurants are too busy and overpriced.

The most beautiful avenue in the world – as it is so often described – was once a meeting place for politicians and war heroes. Now, Avenue des Champs-Élysées is a paradise for shoppers, because not only is it an elegantly tree-lined walking street, it is a place where high-end stores meet high street brands like Zara, Lululemon and Maje.

No matter what you came for, you don't need to compete with the Paris elite to enjoy this impressive avenue. After all, window shopping – or as the French say, *faire du lèche-vitrines* – is free.

"Paris is paramount for fashion, always was – always will be."

Manolo Blahnik, speaking at the Printemps department store opening of the Manolo Blahnik: 40 Years of Glamour exhibition, October 2012

Did You Know?

Working out of an elegant apartment at 31 Rue Cambon, famed couturier **Gabrielle "Coco" Chanel** spent 34 years creating fashion magic in the heart of Paris.

Below it is the original store where she sold No. 5 perfume and for any fashion fan, the address is still a must-visit shopping destination.

Galeries Lafayette

BEST FOR: RAINY DAYS IN PARIS
AREA: LA FAYETTE

Don't Miss... The spectacular views of
Sacré-Cœur from the 18th floor.

Did You Know...? The idea to animate the
window displays at Christmastime originated
as a tribute to Arctic Explorer Robert Peary.

Insider Tip... Macarons in the top-floor
café are some of the finest in Paris!

The "Fashion Capital of the World" owes its enduring reputation to the boom of department stores that made luxury fashion accessible to everyone.

Galeries Lafayette burst onto the high street in 1912 as a luxury bazaar, gradually dominating the corner of Lafayette and Boulevard Haussmann as it expanded upward and outward. Today, it is the leading department store in Europe.

Not only is it popular with tourists – some 37 million a year – but it gets the genuine seal of approval from fashionable locals who will often pop in during their lunch breaks.

Printemps

BEST FOR: LUXURY BRANDS
UNDER ONE ROOF
AREA: LA FAYETTE

Don't Miss... Seventh Heaven – the shop floor dedicated to secondhand designer fashion.

Did You Know...? Printemps opened its first US store in New York in 2025.

Insider Tip... The luxury boutique now accepts cryptocurrencies as payment.

Besides being one of the very first *grand magasins* (large department stores) in Paris back in 1866, Printemps paved the way for ideas like discount sales.

Unsold stock used to go to waste until the newly opened Printemps store advertised their first cut-price event to attract new customers and, in doing so, set a very popular trend.

Today, the department store occupies three prominent locations in Paris, so you'll never be too far away from a Printemps, but the global flagship is ideally situated on the world-class shopping avenue Boulevard Haussmann, a stone's throw from Galeries Lafayette (page 86).

Secret Passageways of Paris

Before shopping centres and department stores, covered shopping alleys were created through Paris to keep shoppers sheltered from the inclement weather.

Not many of the enchanting "Passages Couverts Parisiens" remain, but wherever you still find them, there is a little-known opportunity for vintage treasure hunting and book shopping.

Passage des Panoramas

BEST FOR: ANTIQUES COLLECTING
AREA: BOULEVARD MONTMARTRE

Passage Choiseul

BEST FOR: BOOK LOVERS
AREA: RUE DES PETITS-CHAMPS

Passage du Grand Cerf

BEST FOR: CHARMING BOUTIQUES
AREA: RUE ST DENIS

Galerie Vivienne

BEST FOR: UPMARKET SHOPS
AREA: RUE DES PETITS-CHAMPS

Passage du Havre

BEST FOR: CHRISTMAS SHOPPING
AREA: RUE SAINT-LAZARE

Marché aux Fleurs (Reine Elizabeth II)

BEST FOR: PARISIAN CHARM
AREA: ÎLE DE LA CITÉ

Don't Miss... Beautiful orchids
in all different colours.

Did You Know...? The flower market
was renamed after Queen Elizabeth
II during her 2014 state visit.

Insider Tip... Look but don't touch! Vendors
can be protective over their plants.

The colours, the smells, the sweet chirping of songbirds: it's not hard to see why the Marché aux Fleurs flower market is one of the best-loved shopping experiences in Paris.

In fact, a stroll through these wrought-iron pavilions is so romantic, Queen Elizabeth II visited during her honeymoon here in 1948.

Throughout the week, this 100-year-old market is filled with beautiful bouquets and houseplants. Some people come to buy, others come to photograph the displays or soak up the atmosphere en route to Notre-Dame, thanks to its ideal location.

Best Bookshops

✳ **Shakespeare & Company**
Iconic surrounds, featured in *Midnight in Paris*. (5th Arrondissement)

✳ **Librairie Galignani**
(1st Arrondissement) Chic and elegant browsing in the oldest English-language bookstore on the continent.

✳ **Librairie Delamain**
Step back in history at the oldest bookstore in Paris. (1st Arrondissement)

✳ **The Red Wheelbarrow**
Small and friendly independent bookstore. (6th Arrondissement)

✳ **Librairie OFR**
For high-end art, fashion and design lovers. (3rd Arrondissement)

✳ **The Abbey Bookstore**
For cosy, quaint rummaging in the Latin Quarter. (5th Arrondissement)

✳ **Brentano's**
Beautiful books, artworks and household gifts in Opéra. (9th Arrondissement)

Did You Know?

Copious writers have made
Paris their home and inspiration
over the decades – from French
writers Honoré de Balzac, Victor
Hugo, Marcel Proust and Jean-
Paul Sartre to American greats
Gertrude Stein, Ernest Hemingway
and F. Scott Fitzgerald.

Many of their houses and favourite
cafés can be visited, as well as their
graves at either Père Lachaise
or Montparnasse cemeteries.

CHAPTER FIVE

FOOD & DRINK

Al fresco dining at Les Deux Magots

BEST FOR: PEOPLE WATCHING
AREA: SAINT-GERMAIN-DES-PRÉS

Don't Miss... Gourmet brunches at weekends.

Did You Know...? This is the café where Picasso met his muse Dora Maar.

Insider Tip... Don't just visit in the day. The café hosts jazz concerts every Thursday night.

Dine like Ernest Hemingway and Oscar Wilde at the famous literary café where the Paris elite used to rendezvous throughout the 1930s.

Les Deux Magots is a hop and a skip from Café de Flore, another of Hemingway's favourite spots, and together these two coffee houses popularized the French custom of drinking and socializing (often smoking!) on a café terrace.

Come rain or shine, the most sought-after spots at Les Deux are still the outside tables with chairs facing onto the boulevards, where the combination of fizz-sipping and people watching is second-to-none.

Breakfast at La Maison d'Isabelle

BEST FOR: ALL-BUTTER CROISSANTS
AREA: LATIN QUARTER

Don't Miss... A good thing just because of the queue! It always moves quickly.

Did You Know...? This was the 2018 winner of "best croissant in Paris".

Insider Tip... The bakery is takeaway-only so don't expect a seat with your treat.

You can stop searching for the "best croissants in Paris" because you will find them at La Maison d'Isabelle. Warm, fresh, buttery and flaky: all of the ingredients of the perfect French pastry.

Their award-winning all-butter croissants are made with the highest-quality butter from Charentes-Poitou. And yes, every delicious wheat-flour pastry is, of course, made by hand.

Combine your visit with a walk to Notre-Dame (page 34), only eight minutes north, or the Panthéon (page 38), seven minutes south. Either way, that's just enough time to devour the top-rated croissant in town.

Best Picnic Spots

✳ **Place des Vosges**
The city's oldest public square, surrounded by 17th-century architecture. (4th Arrondissement)

✳ **Jardin des Tuileries**
A centrally located green oasis next to the Seine. (1st Arrondissement)

✳ **Parc des Buttes-Chaumont**
Huge park with playgrounds, temples and a waterfall to explore. (19th Arrondissement)

✳ **Richerand Bridge**
This area of the Canal Saint-Martin is popular with picnicking locals. (10th Arrondissement)

✳ **Jardin de Reuilly**
Modern park with plenty of lawn space. (12th Arrondissement)

✳ **Parc Monceau**
Informal, romantic feel with statues of writers and musicians to discover. (8th Arrondissement)

"Everyone dreams of living in Paris."

Natalie Portman, on her move to France, *Marie Claire* (October 2013)

Escargot at Chez Janou

BEST FOR: TRYING SOMETHING NEW
AREA: LE MARAIS

Don't Miss... The snail pasta.

Did You Know...? It's easier to secure
a table just before 6.30pm, when
the evening food service begins.

Insider Tip... Don't be tempted to seat
yourself in a Paris restaurant. It's customary
to wait for a waiter to show you to a table.

Love it or hate it, eating snails in France is a rite of passage. The most famous way to experience the locals' favourite is straight from the shell with lashings of garlic butter and parsley – a dish known as "escargots de Bourgogne".

At Parisian bistro Chez Janou, they do things a little differently. Instead of serving escargot as a starter course, the French appetizer has been elevated to entrees. Snail pasta, no less.

Food fans rave about the "tagliatelle à la crème aux escargots" as a fresh take on the delicacy or, if you've never tried them before, a more palatable way to taste snails.

Croque Monsieur at Faste

BEST FOR: A TWIST ON A CLASSIC
AREA: SAINT-MARTIN

Don't Miss... The 14-piece selection box for a chance to try every unique croque and side combo.

Did You Know...? A croque madame is a croque monsieur with an egg on top.

Insider Tip... You can order from Faste on most food-delivery services in the city.

Not all Croque Monsieurs are created equal in Paris. So, don't be tempted to try this cheesy sandwich at any tourist hotspot when street-food artisans like Faste are making it the "gourmet" way.

In fact, Faste almost exclusively serves Croque Monsieur. It's their *spécialité*. Over ten finger-licking variations on the traditional sandwich feature on their menus, including a veggie version made with chewy mozzarella, goats cheese instead of gruyere and salmon over ham.

French onion soup at La Jacobine

BEST FOR: TRADITIONAL FRENCH CUISINE
AREA: LATIN QUARTER

Did You Know...? Some say King Louis XV invented the French dish with three ingredients: onions, butter and champagne.

Insider Tip... Ask La Jacobine's knowledgeable waiters for their menu recommendations – they're all too happy to help!

Don't Miss... The hot chocolate for afters.

In the winter, you will be spoilt for rich, delicious comfort food in Paris.

Step inside La Jacobine for a welcome as warming as their celebrated "soupe à l'oignon" (onion soup). A bowl of their home-cooked broth – covered with silky melted cheese – is a highlight of their traditional Parisian-fare menu, which also features favourites like coq au vin, escargot and duck-leg confit.

Late lunches at this cosy bistro feel like an authentic way to spend an afternoon in Paris. Especially when paired with their extensive list of affordable wines.

CHAPTER SIX

ARTS,
MUSIC &
NIGHTLIFE

"I can never decide whether Paris is more beautiful by day or by night."

Marion Cotillard as Adriana, in *Midnight in Paris* (2011)

A Year of Romantic Date Nights

JANUARY Champagne atop the Eiffel Tower

FEBRUARY Dress up for Opéra Garnier

MARCH Cocktails and music at 38 Riv Jazz Club

APRIL Book a classical concert at Sainte-Chapelle

MAY Nuit des Musées for cultured lock-ins

JUNE Tango on the Seine at the riverbank's mini amphitheatres

JULY Admire La Coulée Verte during extended opening hours

AUGUST Picnic under the stars at La Villette's outdoor summer cinema

SEPTEMBER Dinner and dancing on a river cruise along the Seine

OCTOBER See the city lights from the Ponts des Arts

NOVEMBER Wander the Christmas markets

DECEMBER Go ice skating at sunset

Moulin Rouge

BEST FOR: AN IMMERSIVE EXPERIENCE
AREA: MONTMARTRE

Don't Miss... The good seats! Shows
sell out quickly in advance.

Did You Know...? Every show
costume is painstakingly produced
at their dedicated Maisons d'Art.

Insider Tip... Shorts, flip flops and
sportswear are not on the dress code.

When in Paris, the Moulin Rouge is the hottest ticket in town. An institution since 1889, the world's most famous cabaret act is still going strong in Montmartre, attracting hundreds of thousands of annual visitors.

Enter via the iconic red windmills – an unmistakable sight on Place Blanche – and lose yourself in the sequins, feathers and rouge-tinted everything.

If you came for the high-energy and high kicks, you will be blown away by the jaw-dropping talent of the show's 80 dancers, who can do much more than can-can!

The Beautiful Era

Moulin Rouge is one of the most iconic establishments of La Belle Époque (1870–1914) a time when, after two devastating world wars, Parisians experienced a sense of freedom in every sense.

A raft of public theatres, music halls and cabaret venues opened up across France, bringing light-hearted entertainment to wider audiences. Moulin Rouge was colourful, exciting, even a little risqué, but it was fun and it gave the people a new zest for life. A renewed *joie de vivre*.

Peace, Freedom & Prosperity

1878 The first telephone arrives in Paris.

1878 The crowning glory of the Statue of Liberty (her full-size head) goes on display at the Trocadéro before moving to New York.

1885 Louis Pasteur brings pasteurization to the nation.

1889 The Eiffel Tower is unveiled.

1900 The Paris Metro opens.

1900 Grand Palais and Petit Palais open.

1912 Grand opening of Galeries Lafayette.

Opéra Bastille

BEST FOR: SOPHISTICATION
AREA: PLACE DE LA BASTILLE

Don't Miss... Curtain up. Once the performance has started, you won't be granted access to the auditorium.

Did You Know...? Under 28-year-olds get better rates on last-minute tickets.

Insider Tip... Choose fifth row of the Parterre or above for an unobstructed view of the dancers' feet.

There may be two grand opera houses
in the city, but there is only one place
to see the Paris National Opera.

Not only is Opéra Bastille the largest opera
house in Europe (with over 2,000 seats),
it brings music and ballet together under
one roof to make the arts more accessible
to the people of France and its visitors.

The opening in 1989 had huge cultural
significance as it coincided with the 200th
anniversary of the French Revolution (page
54) and was built facing Place de la Bastille,
where the besieged prison once stood.

Bar Hemingway

BEST FOR: COCKTAILS
AREA: PLACE VENDÔME

Don't Miss... The raspberry martinis: strong but delicious.

Did You Know...? The fresh flowers decorating the cocktails symbolize the ladies who made history at this bar.

Insider Tip... The queues can be long, but it's worth the wait.

As if there weren't enough reasons to visit the Ritz Paris, tucked in the corner near the hotel's rear entrance on Rue Cambon is the famous Bar Hemingway, a tiny room with a big reputation.

It quickly became a popular hangout especially after dedicating a section to ladies, who at the time were not allowed to mix with men in bars. Later, Ernest Hemingway became a famous patron and during the hotel bar's 1979 revamp, it was renamed after him.

Today, people don't just come here for the history: it is known to serve some of the best cocktails in town, all within a sumptuous heritage-style setting.

Théâtre Mogador

BEST FOR: MUSICALS
AREA: 9TH ARRONDISSEMENT

Don't Miss... The show! It's recommended that you arrive 45 minutes early.

Did You Know...? The theatre often hosts famous ballets including *Swan Lake*.

Insider Tip... Some shows are in French, but many display English-language subtitles.

From *Cats* and *The Lion King* to *Mamma Mia* and *Beauty & The Beast*, classic family-favourite musicals are laid on with a Parisian twist at Théâtre Mogador.

From your seats, you might notice that the plush red carpets and gilded ceilings are like something out of a West End music hall. It was purposefully designed like this, just off Rue de Londres, in an attempt to draw in British soldiers during World War I.

These days, you're more likely to catch a Broadway musical adapted into French language here. It's a fascinating way to experience the greatest shows – the passion and the emotion tell a powerful story, even if you don't understand a word!

The Birthplace of
Les Misérables

In London's West End, *Les Misérables* became the multi-award-winning, longest-running musical of all time. Despite debuting in (and being written about) Paris in 1980, the show was never well-loved until the songs were rewritten in English.

When the musical recently returned to Paris's Théâtre du Châtelet, the production was translated back to French and it was an instant hit!

"To breathe Paris is to preserve one's soul."

Victor Hugo, *Les Misérables* (1862)

Crazy Horse

BEST FOR: A SEXIER SIDE OF PARIS
AREA: CHAMPS-ÉLYSÉES

Don't Miss... Last-minute tickets at the venue on the day of the show. Sometimes they're the best value.

Did You Know...? Some of the routines have been used since it opened in the 1950s.

Insider Tip... For the best tables, buy a bottle of champagne with your seats.

Late nights in the City of Lights are best spent at the infamous Crazy Horse. It's a cabaret experience like no other in town, exhibiting an even sexier side – if you can believe it – to the Moulin Rouge (page 114).

The thrill of a 90-minute show here could include burlesque, contortionism, aerial routines, or even tasteful striptease, so needless to say, it's nothing short of wild.

In the light of day, the venue might stand out beside the Balenciaga boutique and Givenchy HQ, but on an evening out, it's ideally located for all the trendy bars of the Champs-Élysées.

"We'll always have Paris."

Humphrey Bogart as Rick Blaine in
Casablanca (1942)